Espionage Mechanism in the Arthasastra of Kautilya
Ratan Lal Basu

Espionage Mechanism in the Arthasastra of Kautilya

Ratan Lal Basu

Published by Kautilya, 2023.

Espionage Mechanism in Arthasastra of Kautilya

ESPIONAGE MECHANISM IN THE ARTHASASTRA OF KAUTILYA

First edition. February 8, 2023.

Copyright © 2023 Ratan Lal Basu.

ISBN: 979-8215778890

Written by Ratan Lal Basu.

Contents

Chapter-1: Espionage in Arthaśāstra - Internal

Introduction

Espionage has been an inexorable part of statecraft ever since the emergence of state as the supreme institution of governance of human societies. The term espionage, in general, applies to both internal intelligence of a state and intelligence pertaining to other countries. The ruler or ruling institutions of the state have to be well informed of the internal situation of a country, its citizens, the internal rival groups or individuals, the dissidents, the supporters of the ruling institution or ruler, the groups or individuals striving to destabilize the state machinery or conspiring against the government; the various conflicting groups and the inner struggle among them, the designs and movements of criminals of various categories, problems and aspirations of the people belonging to various social categories and professions etc. The quality and efficiency of governance of a state unquestionably depends on the quantity and quality of intelligence on the above mentioned aspects. In fact, without a competent internal espionage network, it is well neigh impossible for the government of a country to rule properly.

Quality of governance depends a good deal on the quality of internal intelligence. On the other hand the state ought to be well aware of the other countries – friendly, neutral and enemy countries – interstate rivalry or coalition, the attitude of them towards the country concerned, their war efforts, and weaponry, internal situation of these countries and their citizens, their economic conditions etc. All these pertain to external intelligence which has two aspects, viz. espionage activities about other countries that include both gathering of intelligence about them and destabilizing them in case of the enemy countries and to protect the country from espionage onslaughts of other countries (counter-espionage).

Two most important external activities of a state, ever since its emergence, have been to protect itself from foreign invasion and espionage plays a crucial role in facilitating successful external defence and territorial expansion by captivating other countries. No war, either a defensive or an offensive, could be waged successfully without high quality external intelligence as well as counter-intelligence. The basic characteristics of the states have remained almost unchanged even today notwithstanding the global efforts towards avoiding war and conflicts and emergence of world bodies like the UNO, the World Bank, and the WTO etc. Imperialism has changed forms in course of time from open to clandestine, indirect economic imperialism instead of direct territorial occupation, and in many cases hot war has changed into cold war without direct use of destructive weapons. So, importance of external intelligence has remained the same in statecraft in modern days. Moreover, economic intelligence networks to unravel economic secrets of other countries and to steal technologies from other countries have become common practice in the modern world.

With the progress of theories pertaining to state and material progress, complexities of inter-state relations have increased in course of time and accordingly, external espionage has become more complex and sophisticated. Keeping pace with the evolution of communication technologies, especially cyber technology, espionage techniques have become more and more subtle and complicated and opportunities to utilize modern technologies have added new dimensions to modern espionage and counter espionage theories. Spectacular developments of technologies pertaining to arms and ammunitions and destructive power of weaponry have enhanced the importance of mrlitary intelligence and counter intelligence of each country. Now-a-days, an important aspect of external intelligence pertains to weaponry and war efforts of other countries. With spectacular advance of productive technologies and technological gap between technologically advanced and backward countries, industrial and economic espionage has emerged as a novel aspect of modern external espionage. This pertains to both purely economic and war related technologies. Cyber technology has added new dimensions to modern espionage and cyber espionage (through Hacking, Phishing, Trojan horse and other similar devices) is something completely new in the arena of espionage.

The science of espionage has a long history of evolution and probably it originated ever since the emergence of state as the supreme form of governance in clan societies. The science, in course of emergence of larger states achieved high level of development in Egypt, Syria, Persia, China, Greece and India. By the 4th century B. C. the science of espionage in India achieved a spectacular level of advancement which was incorporated in Arthaśāstra. The basic theories of espionage as prescribed by Kauṭilya have changed very little in course of the last two millennia and three hundred years notwithstanding the widespread use of technological devices developed in course of industrial advance, especially, the cyber technology developed in course of the last few decades. As regards effectiveness of espionage methods, the modern espionage agencies are yet to learn a lot from the theories and practices of espionage as embodied in Arthaśāstra.

The major topics covered in this chapter are:
Essence of Arthaśāstra Espionage: Human Vices and Weaknesses
Types of Spies and Their Functions
Test of Ministers and Government Officials
Punishing Treasonable Officials by Devious Means
Stratagem against Princes or Officials Going to Join the Enemy
Dangers from Officers in the Outer Region and the Interior
Spy Network for the Citizens
Apprehending and Punishing Criminals
Essence of Arthaśāstra Espionage: Human Vices and Weaknesses
Kauṭilya's espionage method was mainly based on use of human resources which in modern parlance may be termed 'Humint'. Kauṭilya's supremacy lies in the fact that his espionage theory had in its essence

basic vices and vulnerabilities of human beings. Kauṭilya had a thorough knowledge of the ancient Indian concept of the innermost aspects of human psychosis from which all conceivable human vices and vulnerabilities arise.

Basic human modes – the Sankhya concepts (Ballantyne, 1885)

According to Sankhya philosophy of Kapila of ancient India, human nature and consciousness is a combination of three basic modes, viz. satva, rajasa and tamasa (the adjectives of these abstract nouns are respectively sātvika, rājasika and tāmasika). If isolated in the abstract, unmixed satva pertains to goodness and virtue, rajasa to passion and insatiable desire and tamasa to darkness of mind, obsession and inertia. All our mental and intellectual faculties originate from these three basic modes. All these basic modes combine in different degrees to assign different characteristics to different individuals.

These three classes of people in the pure form may be distinguished on the basis of certain baser and nobler human attributes. The baser features are found in the highest degree and nobler ones in the lowest degree in a tāmasika person. For the rājasika person, both types of features are of moderate degree; and for the sātvika, nobler qualities are found in the highest degree and baser ones are completely absent.

The ṛpus or basic human instincts1

Now let us take up another concept from ancient Indian texts, viz. the concept of ṛpus. Literally ṛpu means enemy, but as used in ancient Indian texts these basic instincts of human psychology are not enemies as such. They are inexorable parts of biological existence of human beings and turn into enemies only if uncontrolled. There are six ṛpus, viz. kāma (desire for material pleasure/lust), krodha (anger), lobha (greed), moha (delusion), mada (pride/vanity), mātsarya (jealousy/envy).

The basic instincts, pertaining to the ṛpus, can be used for good or bad, but by themselves they are neutral. If the basic instincts are kept under control, they are always beneficial, but if they get the better of us, they turn into enemies and ruin us in the short or long run.

The ṛpus take various major forms under different modes.

For a sātvika person ṛpus are fully controlled and turn out to be benign.

For a rājasika person, kāma in the narrow sense takes the form of preoccupation with sensual pleasure, and in the wider sense it leads to insatiable craving for power and wealth (by just or unjust means); krodha takes the form of secret planning and conspiracy for taking reprisals; lobha gets associated with achieving all sorts of material pleasures, power, fame etc.; moha makes him always pre-occupied with the fruits of his works and activities; mada and mātsarya goad him to desperate and restless activity in order to supersede all his superiors.

For a tāmasika person kāma is associated with perverse and brutal sexual desire, forceful violation of the opposite sex, incest and unnatural sex behaviour. His krodha is blind and destructive, both for others and for himself; his lobha centers on all conceivable dirty and shabby pleasures – addictions to drugs, alcohol etc. For him, mada leads to false vanity and day-dreaming; moha is full of superstitions, baseless knowledge and inactivity; mātsarya burns his soul and goads him to inflict harm on others. The espionage theory of Kauṭilya had in its basis the basic modes and instincts of human mind. Emphasis was laid on categorization of all relevant target persons (ministers and government officials, queens and concubines, princes and princesses, all categories of citizens of both the own country and foreign countries including kings of foreign countries) on the basis of modes and ṛpus [The Devi Bhagavatam- 7.35.2-3 (book-7, chapter-35, ślokas -2-3)] and exploiting their vulnerabilities with appropriate means. Pure sātvika persons are not at all vulnerable, but in real world they are very rare. Most real world people, because of their tāmasika and rājasika traits and uncontrolled ṛpus, are vulnerable somewhere. The task of the spies is to identify the vulnerable aspect of each target and explore its vulnerability by applying suitable means, e.g., women for lusty persons, money for greedy persons, enticement of power for the proud and for the obsessed ones, superstition, magic, occult practices, miracles etc. In this regard the agent provocateur has a crucial role in Kauṭilya's methods of espionage.

Types of Spies and Their Functions

Types of spies

Kauṭilya revealed extraordinary insight and skill in selecting and appointing spies that are to penetrate and get assimilated with every sphere of society in the protagonist's own country and in foreign countries (friendly, inimical or neutral).

Kauṭilya classified the spies to be appointed into the following major categories:

i) Sharp pupil

ii) Apostate monk

iii) Seeming householder

iv) Seeming trader

v) Seeming ascetic

vi) Secret agent

vii) Bravo

viii) Poison giver

ix) Begging nun

Each category of spies is assigned specific tasks.

Now let us take up the details of these various types of secret agents or spies.

Kauṭilya emphasizes to start with that after uprightness of the ministers being assured by means of secret tests, the king should appoint persons in secret service – the sharp pupil, the apostate monk, the seeming householder, the seeming trader and the seeming ascetic, the secret agent called the bravo, the poison-giver and the begging nun.

Definitions of the spies belonging to the above categories

i) Sharp pupil

A sharp pupil is a student or disciple who is intelligent, loyal, patriotic and also courageous.

He should have knowledge of the secrets of others and should be bold. He would be encouraged with money and honour, and the minister dealing with him should instruct that he is to regard the king and the minister as authority, and report to them at once any evil of any person he happens to come upon.

ii) Apostate monk

The wandering monk, who has relinquished monkhood, is loyal and looking for job is to be picked up and appointed in the category of apostate monk. Only those monks who have been tested to have intelligence and whose honesties have been assured through appropriate tests are to be taken up for appointing as apostate monks.

He would be provided with money and other accessories necessary for discharging the duties he is entrusted with. Equipped with plenty of money and assistants, the apostate monk should maintain secrecy under the guise of some occupation.

From the profits of the work assigned to the apostate monk for his guise, the minister in charge of this category of spies should bear the expenses of the wandering monks pertaining to food, clothing and residence.

For those of the monks who seek a permanent livelihood, the minister should arrange for such jobs and advise them to work under the garb of the job for the interest of the king and present himself with collected secret reports to the appointer at the time of meals and receiving salaries.

New wandering monks are to be recruited through the existing monks – the existing monk spies are to be advised to propose other monks in similar position to join the service of the king as apostate monks.

iii) Seeming householder

An intelligent and honest farmer whose source of income from agriculture has depleted and therefore he is obliged to look for a job is to be appointed in the seeming household category.

He would be assigned with profitable agricultural land and under the guise of a householder subsiding from agricultural pursuits he would discharge his duties as a spy. This person would be in a position to have information of other households and farmers around the place of work he is appointed at.

iv) Seeming trader

Just like the farmer, an intelligent and honest trader whose source of income from trade has depleted and therefore he is obliged to look for a job is to be appointed in the seeming trader category. He would be appointed in trading activities at some place desirable by the minister for gathering information. Under the guise of a trader he would collect secret information about all traders around him and pass this on to the minister controlling him.

v) Seeming ascetic

Spying activities would also be done through agents under the guise of hermits residing in the vicinity of the city. Those hermits (practitioner of religious rites with shaven heads or with matted hair) who want to relinquish their practices as hermits and are desirous of getting permanent government jobs would be appointed in the category of spies known as seeming ascetic. The major task of a seeming hermit would be to find out loyal and intelligent employees for the government, gather information about people having discontent and grudges against the king and pacify them by various means.

A spy of this category would be installed in the vicinity of the city and he should attract disciples who are willing to accept him as guru. He should impress everyone by openly eating only a vegetable or a handful of barley at intervals of a month or two (secretly, however, he would take meals as desired by him).

To impress people about his supernatural power through occult practices, spies under the guise of traders should make open announcement that they could achieve prosperity in business by means of the occult practices of the hermit.

His disciples should also make open announcement to everyone that this holy hermit is capable of bringing about prosperity to anyone seeking his supernatural assistance. It is natural that people would approach the hermit for securing prosperity in various spheres of life. Thereafter, to those who approach the hermit with hopes of securing prosperity, he should specify events happening in their families, which are ascertained by means of the science of interpreting the touch of the body and with the help of signs made by his disciples, events such as small gain, burning by fire, danger from thieves, the killing of a treacherous person, a gift of gratification, news about happenings in a foreign land, saying, 'this will happen today or tomorrow,' or 'the king will do this.'

After these announcements, the secret agents associated with the hermit would cause the prophecies of the hermit to be realized. This would make the seekers of prosperity highly impressed by the supernatural prowess of the hermit.

Now, to those among the visitors who are richly endowed with spirit, intelligence and eloquence, he should predict good fortune at the hands of the king and speak of their imminent association with the minister. Thereafter, the relevant minister would arrange for their employment and livelihood.

As regards those who are resentful for reasonable causes, he should convince them and pacify them with money, honour and other rewards. However, he should bring under control through secret punishment and fear psychosis, those persons who are resentful or inimical to the king without any reason, or are engaged in harmful activities against the king.

These spies under the guise of occult hermits are also to be entrusted with the responsibility of ascertaining the integrity of the state employees.

vi) Secret agent

A person, to be appointed in the category of secret agent, should have thorough knowledge of magic and occult practices, fortune telling, astrology etc. so that he can befool or trap gullible people and extract information from them. These secret agents should be free from family attachments. They are to be experts in Atharvavedic practices or black arts and capable of studying the psychology of common people. They should also be capable of making people impressed by their practice of magic, generating illusion among people and thereby collecting secret information from the enchanted people.

vii) Bravo

Some people are intrepid, desperate and adventurous by nature, capable of fighting like mercenaries, have no sentimental attachments, rejoice taking risks and care a fig for their own lives. These desperadoes are to be selected for the category of bravo. This type of intrepid people if desirous of earning money could be utilized (by temptation of money) to undertake very risky activities necessary at times for the security and proper functioning of the state machinery.

viii) Poison giver

Persons who have no affections for kinsmen or other people, and are cruel and malicious by nature are to be appointed as poison givers.

ix) Begging nun

The wandering nuns, (with shaven head and commanding reverence from religious and superstitious people), who are seeking livelihood are to be picked up and appointed in the category of begging nun. They are to be selected from among those who are poor, widowed, bold, Brāhmaṇa by caste and treated with honour in the king's palace and have access to the houses of high officials of the king. So, all information about the activities of the high level government officials, their fidelity or deceitful nature could be ascertained through these begging nuns.

Confirmation by three spies

For each mission, three spies, unknown to one another, would be appointed for confirmation of reports from the spies and prevent mistakes or deliberate cheating/lying by spies. If reports of each of them match, it would be accepted as confirmed. In case reports vary, further checks should be made to detect if one or more spies had made mistakes or cheated deliberately. Once detected the miscreant/miscreants would be punished and removed from his/their job/jobs. Moreover, the knowledge to each spy that there are other spies around him to report about his activities, would compel him to refrain from giving false information.

Salaries of spies

Salaries of various categories of spies as delineated in Arthaśāstra could be evaluated only in relative terms. Absolute assessment is not possible because it is not possible to convert the major currency (paṇa) in circulation at Kauṭilya's time into rupee or any other modern currency. The salaries of the major categories of spies and secret agents, according to Arthaśāstra guidelines, are:

Sharp pupil, Apostate monk, Seeming householder, Seeming trader and Seeming ascetic = 1000 paṇas

Secret agent, Poison-giver and Begging nun = 500 paṇas

Functions of spies

Various categories of spies are to be employed with trustworthy disguises, disguise as regards country, dress, profession, language and birth. As regards all these aspects there should be perfection so that no body is capable of suspecting the status they openly declare.

These spies would be assigned tasks in conformity with their intelligence, loyalty, and capability of gathering correct information without being detected or raising any suspicion in the victim/victims. The persons under surveillance of the spies would be all the employees of the king including the councilor, the chaplain, the commander-in-chief, the crown-prince, the chief palace usher, the chief of the palace guards, the administrator, the director of stores, the magistrate, the commandant, the city-judge, the director of factories, the council of ministers, the superintendents, the chief of the army staff, the commandant of the fort, the commandant of the frontier-fort and the forest chieftain.

Bravoes, serving as bearers of umbrella, water-vessel, fan, shoes, seat and carriage and riding animals, would be entrusted with spying on and ascertaining the out-of-door activities of the officials mentioned above. They should pass on the information collected by them to the secret agents who should communicate that information to the spy establishments.

The indoor activities of these officials are to be spied upon and ascertained by spies under the guise of cooks, waiters, bath-attendants, shampooers, bed-preparers, barbers, valets and water-servers, those appearing as hump-backs, dwarfs, hunters, dumb, deaf, idiotic or blind persons, and actors, dancers, singers, musicians, professional story-tellers and minstrels. Begging nuns should collect information of indoor activities of the officials from all these spies and pass the information on to the spy establishments.

Assistants of the spy establishments should carry out the transmission of spied out news by means of various signs and symbols. Neither the establishments nor these assistants should know one another.

In case of prohibition of entry into the houses of the officials for begging nuns, secret agents appearing at the door one after another or appearing as the mother or father of servants in the house, or posing as female artists, singers or female slaves, should collect the secret information from the spies employed inside the houses with the help of various secret means – songs and recitations bearing secret information, writings concealed in musical instruments or symbols and signs.

Another means of passing out secret information is that a get-away from the house should be made secretly by the spies by taking advantage of pretended long illness or madness or by setting something on fire or administering poison to someone.

Test of Ministers and Government Officials

i) Ministers

Integrity of ministers is to be tested by unraveling their susceptibility to different ṛpus (lust, anger, greed, pride, delusion and jealousy) and they should be assigned responsibility for departments where their weaknesses and vulnerabilities would not be harmful.

After appointment of ministers to ordinary offices in consultation with the conciliators and the chaplain, the king should test their integrity by means of secret test. The test is to be taken through agent provocateurs.

To start with a got up misunderstanding between the king and the chaplain would be arranged and the king would seemingly discard the chaplain under some pretext.

Thereafter spies as agent provocateurs would approach each minister individually and goad him with suggestions that by discharging the chaplain the king has violated moral norms and so he is impious and ought to be removed from power and replaced by some pious person either belonging to the royal family or a foreign prince or any other suitable person. The spies should insist that the other ministers have already agreed to remove the king and now they hope that the minister concerned has the same view. If the minister disagrees to accept the suggestions of the spies he would be considered loyal.

In the same way the king would seemingly dismiss the commander of the army who, thereafter would try to provoke each minister through agent provocateurs with offers of money and other material gains in the same fashion as above to seek his compliance with the conspiracy to destroy the king. Like the previous case, if the minister reacts negatively to the proposal, he would be taken to be honest, loyal, upright and free from material temptations.

The vulnerability of the ministers to lust and women would be tested through the wandering nuns. A wandering nun, who has won the confidence of different ministers and is treated with honour in the palace, should secretly suggest to each minister individually that the chief queen is in love with him and has made arrangements for a secret meeting with him.

If the minister concerned repulses the proposal, his purity as regards women and lust would be substantiated.

By various similar methods through agent provocateurs the king would be able to ascertain the loyalty and also weaknesses and vulnerabilities of the ministers.

Now, from among the ministers tested and proved loyal in one or more respects, the king should appoint them on the basis of the nature of their loyalty and uprightness. Those proved loyal by the test of piety are to be appointed to posts in the judiciary and for oppression of criminals, those proved upright by the test of material gain to offices of the administrator and in the stores of the director of stores, those proved pure by the test of lust to guardianship of places of recreation inside the palace as well as outside.

The king should appoint the ministers who have been proved loyal and honest by all the tests, as his councilors.

Those found dishonest by every test, are to be employed in mines, in forests for material produce, in elephant-forests and in factories.

ii) Departmental heads

Activities of all departmental heads and other officials in similar position should be brought under strict surveillance of the spies. If any officer spends more than his income, it is certain that he is dishonest and his additional spending is at the cost of state revenue. Spies would be entrusted with the task of ascertaining this type of dishonesty of the officers.

iii) Village officials

The king, through spy administrators, should station in the country side secret agents under the guise of holy ascetics, wandering monks, cart-drivers, wandering minstrels, jugglers, tramps, fortune-tellers, soothsayers, astrologers, physicians, lunatics, dumb persons, deaf persons, idiots, blind persons, traders, artisans, artists, actors, brothel-keepers, dealers in bread, dealers in cooked meat, and dealers in cooked rice and various other professions.

These spies under various guises would be entrusted with the responsibility of ascertaining integrity or unscrupulousness of village-officers.

If any officer is suspected by the spies to be of questionable income (income beyond what he ought to earn from legal sources), he should be kept under strict vigilance by spies in order to find out the source of his secret and illegal income.

The secret agents should also act as agent provocateurs to test the honesty or otherwise of the village officers. The procedure is like this: an agent provocateur should say to a village officer that some rouge with plenty of wealth is in trouble and taking advantage of his difficult position the officer ought to extort money from him. If the officer falls into this trap and agrees to do so, he would be considered as an extortionist and dismissed from job.

Similar provoking methods should be applied on all rural officers to check their integrity and proneness to corruption.

iv) Judges and magistrates

A secret agent who has gained confidence of a judge should request the judge to accept bribe and give judgement in favour of some person who is a relative of him and is an accused before the judge concerned. If the judge agrees to accept bribe and release the accused (non-existent) as mentioned by the agent he should be considered as a dishonest judge and dismissed from his position.

Punishing Treasonable Officials by Devious Means

Sometimes the treachery and unscrupulousness of the officers may be felt to be certain, but because of their cunning these guilt cannot be proved openly. In this case it is not possible to punish the miscreant openly. In such a case these cunning officials are to be punished by secret means through the spy network.

i) Through the kinsmen of the miscreant

1. A secret agent, after inciting a brother of the treasonable high officer, not honoured by him, should induce him to fight against the treasonable officer with the assurance that he would get the king's assistance to snatch his property. When the brother has acted with a weapon or poison as suggested by the spies, the latter should assassinate him and pass on the blame to the treasonable officer creating the evidence on the basis of which he could be executed for killing his brother.

2. A brother, instigated by a secret agent, should demand inheritance from the treasonable officer. As he lies down at the door of the treasonable man's house at night, or when he is staying elsewhere, an assassin, slaying him, should declare, 'this claimant of the inheritance is killed.' Then, giving support to the slain man's party, the king should suppress the treasonable officer.

3. Secret agents, staying near the treasonable officer, should threaten the brother claiming inheritances with death. Thereafter the action would be as in the previous case.

4. When of two treasonable officers, a son has relations with the father's wife or a father with the son's wife or a brother with that of a brother, started by a secret agent would instigate a fight between the two and get both the fighting parties executed as in the preceding manner – i.e., in course of the fight the secret agent would secretly kill one of the contenders and pass the blame on the other.

5. A secret agent should instigate a son of the treasonable officer thinking highly of himself, suggesting 'you are really the king's son, kept here through fear of enemy.'

When he believes that, the king should honour him in private by saying, 'though the time for installing you as the crown prince has come, I am not crowning you through fear of the officer.'

The secret agent should induce him to murder the officer.

When he has acted, the king should cause him to be executed on that very ground, declaring, 'he is a patricide.'

6. A female mendicant agent, having won the confidence of the wife of the treasonable officer by means of love-winning potions, should cheat him by the use of poison.

ii) Miscellaneous devious stratagem

1. An agent appearing as a holy man should make the officer, who has faith in black magic believe, by saying, that he could attain his goal by performing some occult rite. When he undertakes to perform the rite, the spy under the guise of holy man should get him killed in the course of the rite by poison announcing, 'he was killed by a mishap in the rite.'

2. An agent appearing as a physician, after establishing a malignant or incurable disease for the treasonable person, should cheat him with poison in the preparations of medicine or food.

3. Agents, employed as cooks or food servers, should cheat the treasonable person by means of poison.

4. Assassins should set fire to the fields, threshing-floors or houses, or bring down their weapons on the kinsmen, relations or draught-animals of those treasonable persons whose mutual quarrels are deep-rooted, and say, 'we were engaged by so and so.'

For that offence the others should be punished.

5. Secret agents should induce treasonable officers in the fortified city and in the country to be one another's guests. In the occasion, one or more of the officers would be killed by poison givers and the spies would pass the blame on the other officers who would then be punished for poisoning fellow officers.

6. A spy under the guise of a female mendicant should suggest a treasonable chief in the country that the wife, the daughter-in-law or the daughter of another chief in is in love with the former. If this chief falls into the trap and agrees to encounter the female concerned, the spy with some evidence of his acceptance (for example, gifts offered by the chief), would inform the other chief of the mischievous intentions of the former chief.

In this way the spy would cause a quarrel between the two and taking advantage of the confusion of quarrel the spy would kill one and pass on the blame to the other who would then be punished for killing his fellow officer.

Stratagem against Princes or Officials Going to Join the Enemy

When princes or high officials try to join the enemy camp the spies are to create distrust and enmity between the two sides (those attempting to join hand with enemies and the enemies) through continuous propaganda to each against the other. The first attempt of the spies would be to win back the princes or other officials opting for joining the enemy camp by pleading that the enemies are going only to use them to serve their designs and once these are fulfilled they would kill the renegade princes or officials. If they could be won back it is well and good. But if all these efforts fail and they are still adamant to join the enemy camp, the secret agents should arrange for killing them through assassins.

The secret agents should also endeavour to win back the soldiers who had left along with the princes or high officials by means of offering them various concessions.

Dangers from Officers in the Outer Region and the Interior

Danger to the kingdom may arise from connivance between officers posted in the outer region and those posted in the interior region of the country. Under such circumstances the secret agents are to adopt the following measures to nullify the conspiracy hatched jointly by outer and inner officials. The basic endeavour of the spies would be to generate dissension and mistrust between the two conspiring parties.

1. Secret agents, posing as friends of those in the outer regions should communicate to them the following secret information, 'this king intends to overreach you through these posing as treasonable men; beware.'

2. Secret agents, posing as treasonable men, employed with the treasonable men in the interior, should divide the treasonable men in the

interior from those in the outer regions or posing as allies of treasonable men in the exterior divide them from those in the interior region.

3. Assassins may be deployed to get mixed as seemingly allies of both groups of treasonable men and kill them secretly by means of poison or weapons.

4. Posing as allies of the conspirators in the outer regions and inviting them to the capital, the secret assassins should kill them.

5. Secret agents, posing as friends of the conspirators in both the regions should remind them the power of the king to detect conspiracy and warn them by saying that the king has already become aware of his designs and would soon take punitive measures against him and therefore it would be better for him to eschew the path of conspiracy and treason.

6. Assassins, insinuating themselves in the troops of the envoy of the one responding, should strike at their weak points with weapon, poison and so on. Then secret agents should accuse the one responding for that crime.

7. An agent posing as a friend, should say to them, 'in order to find out your feelings, the king will put you to test; you should disclose them to him.'

8. Secret agents should divide the treasonable officials from one another saying, 'so and so is thus whispering to the king about you'.

Spy Network for the Citizens

Popularizing the king among the citizens

Along with the espionage network for the government officials, the king should also undertake to set up a vast and all-embracing spy network for citizens belonging to all walks of life.

One of the major tasks of the spies would be to make the king popular among the citizens and to inspire respect and awe among the citizens about the king. Propaganda in an indirect way should be made by the secret agents about the power and various extraordinary attributes of the king.

Spies, apparently opposing one another, should carry on debate at various places characterized by large public gatherings, e.g., holy places, markets, and other congregations of people.

One of the spies seemingly against the king would openly blame the king of having no virtues which he claims to possess. Then the other spy opposing the first one would explain that this idea of the first spy is a misunderstanding and would explain clearly why the king in fact possesses divine attributes and the wellbeing and security of each citizen depends on the king. So, the king should be revered by each and every one. In this way, through open debates and discussions the king should be popularized among the citizens by the spies.

Gathering information about the attitude of common people

The spies should find out all the rumours that are spreading among the citizens of the country.

Spies appearing as ascetics with shaven heads or with matted hair should ascertain the contentedness or discontentedness of the citizens, and their roles to do beneficial or harmful activities for the country. Spies appearing as fortune-tellers, soothsayers and astrologers would get closer to the citizens, should ascertain their mutual relations as well as their contacts with enemies or forest chieftains.

The king should favour those who are contented, with additional wealth and honour. He should propitiate with gifts and conciliation those, who are discontented, in order to make them contented.

Those who are enraged or greedy or frightened or proud, are likely to be seduced by enemies. The secret agents should detect these persons and the king should be cautious of these persons who are likely to create trouble.

In this way, the wise king should guard from the secret instigations of enemies, those likely to be seduced and those not likely to be seduced in his own territory, whether prominent person or common people.

Spies stationed at various places

i) At trading check posts

Close to the flag of the tax collection point spies are to be installed to detect attempts by traders to evade tolls and taxes. The secret agents are to detect if goods have passed beyond the foot of the flag without the duty being paid and on the basis of the findings the trader involved would be liable to pay the fine amounting to eight times the duty evaded.

Or a secret agent appearing as a trader should communicate to the king the size of the caravan of traders and other details pertaining to the commodities in the caravan.

In accordance with that information, the king should tell the collector of customs about the size of the caravan, in order to make his power of omniscience known to the collector. Thereafter the collector, on meeting the caravan, should verify this detail from the traders concerned. Once verified, both the collector and the traders would be convinced about the power of the king and start believing that nothing could be kept out of the sight of the king with his omniscience and therefore would never attempt to cheat the king by evading duties.

ii) At ale houses

The king should take initiative in constructing ale-houses consisting of many rooms, and provided with separate beds and seats for the customers. There would also be drinking bars provided with perfumes, flowers and water, and pleasant in all seasons.

Secret agents, placed there, should ascertain the normal and occasional expenditure of customers and get information about strangers.

They should make a note of ornaments, clothes and cash of customers who are intoxicated or sleeping. In case of loss of these, the owner of the ale house should compensate the loss and pay a fine of equal amount to the loss for negligence or involvement in stealing.

Owners, on their part, should appoint beautiful female servants to gather information about the intensions of the customers of all categories through direct association with them and also when they are intoxicated or asleep in secluded parts of the rooms. iii) At brothels

Prostitutes and their sons would be trained to work as spies and pass on information about the designs and other details of the customers visiting the brothels.

iv) On roads

Secret agents operating along roads and away from roads should arrest, outside the city and inside, in temples, holy places, forests and cremation grounds all suspected persons, e.g., a person with a wound, one with harmful tools, one hiding behind a heavy load, one agitated, one in a long sleep, one tired after a journey or a stranger.

v) At deserted places

Inside the city, the secret agents under various guises, in order to find out secret or criminal activities, should make a search in deserted places, work-shops, ale-houses, cooked-rice houses, cooked-meat houses, gambling dens and quarters of heretics.

Functions of various categories of spies

i) Seeming householders

Agents in the guise of householders, directed by the administrator, should find out the number of fields, houses and families in those villages in which they are stationed – fields with respect to their size and total produce, houses with respect to taxes and exemptions and families with respect to their caste and occupation.

Moreover, they should find out the number of individuals in each family and their income and expenditure. These spies should also find out the reason for departure and stay of those who have gone on a journey and those who have arrived respectively, as also of men and women who are harmful.

ii) Seeming traders

Spies in the guise of traders should find out the quantity and price of the king's goods produced in his own country, obtained from mines, water-works, forests, factories and fields.

iii) Seeming ascetics

Secret agents posing as ascetics should ascertain the honesty or dishonesty of farmers, cowherds and traders and of the departmental heads.

iv) Old thieves

Old thieves who have eschewed the path of stealing and sought job from the government would be employed as spies to gather information about the thieves and similar miscreants. They should find out the reasons for entry, stay and departures of thieves and brave men of the enemy in sanctuaries, cross-roads, deserted places, wells, rivers, pools, river crossings, temple compounds, hermitages, jungles, mountains, forests and thickets.

Apprehending and Punishing Criminals

i) False witnesses

An agent pretending to be an accused should coax with bribe persons suspected to be false witnesses to help them with false testimony. If they agree to do so, they should be exiled as false witnesses.

ii) Black magic practitioners

If the spy considers any one as a user of occult means for winning love with incantations or rites with herbs or rites in cremation grounds, he should say to the suspect, 'I am in love with wife, daughter in law or daughter of so and so; make her reciprocate my love and take this money.'

If he agrees to do so, he should be exiled as a user of occult means for winning love.

iii) Illegal dealers of poisons

If the spy suspects anyone of preparing, purchasing or selling poison, he should say to the suspect, 'so and so is my enemy; bring about his death and take this money.'

If he consents to do so, he should be exiled as a poison-giver.

iv) Dealer of counterfeit coins

If the spy suspects anyone as a dealer of counterfeit coins, being a frequent purchaser of various metals and acids, of coals, bellows, pincers, vices, anvils, dies, chisels and crucibles, with indications of hands and clothes smeared with soot, ashes and smoke, and being possessed of blacksmith's tools, the spy should expose him by insinuating himself into his confidence as a pupil and by carrying on dealings with him.

If exposed, he should be exiled as a dealer of false coins.

v) Persons earning by causing injury to others

Persons, having secret ways of income, by causing injury to others, should be exposed by the secret agents and exiled or they should pay a redemption-amount in accordance the gravity of the offence.

vi) Robbers and forest criminals

1. Secret agents posing as friends of robbers should cause a herd of cattle or a caravan in the vicinity of a forest to be destroyed by the robbers.

And making the food and drink placed there, in accordance with an agreement, mixed with a stupefying liquid, they should go away.

Then cowherds and traders should cause the robbers carrying loads of stolen goods to be attacked when the stupefying liquid is having its effect.

2. An agent appearing as an ascetic with shaven head or with matted locks and posing as a devotee of god Saṁkarṣaṇa, should overreach the forest robbers by using a stupefying liquid after holding a festival. Then he should with his men attack and apprehend the robbers.

3. An agent appearing as a vintner should overreach forest criminals by using a stupefying liquid on the occasion of the sale or presentation of wine during festivities in honour of gods or funeral rites or festive gatherings. Once the liquid starts working the spy with his men should attack the criminals and apprehend them.

4. After scattering in many groups the forest tribes that have come for plundering the town, the spy should destroy each isolated group.

vii) Outwitting the criminals

Secret agents appearing as holy men should entice criminals by means of lores favourite with them, viz., robbers by means of charms inducing sleep, making invisible or opening doors, adulterers by love-winning charms.

When the robbers have been enthused to see the power of the charms, the spies should take a large band of the robbers at night and proposing to go to one village should go to another village in which men and women are prepared beforehand, and say, 'right here you can see the power of our lore; it is difficult to go to the other village.'

Then opening the gates by means of a gate-opening charm, they should say, 'enter.'

By means of an invisibility charm they should make the criminals go safely through the midst of wakeful guards.

Sending guards to sleep with a sleep-inducing charm they should cause them with their beds to be moved by the criminals.

With a love-winning charm they should make the criminals enjoy harlots appearing as other men's wives.

When the robbers are convinced of the power of their lores, the spies should prescribe the performance of preliminary rites and so on, so that they may be recognized.

Or, the spies should induce the criminals to steal in houses in which goods have been marked.

Or, they should get the criminals caught in one place after winning their confidence.

The spies should get the criminals arrested while engaged in purchasing, selling or pledging articles that are marked or when they are intoxicated with drugged liquor.

When the criminals are arrested, the spies should question them concerning former offences and their associates.

Or, secret agents appearing as old thieves should, after winning their confidence, get thieves to do their work in the same manner and get them arrested.

When they are arrested, the administrator should point them out to citizens and country people, saying, 'The king has studied the lore of catching thieves; it is under his instruction that these thieves have been caught; I shall catch others too; you should therefore restrain your kinsmen who may have criminal tendencies.'

And if the administrator were to come to know through the information of the spies that someone among them has stolen a trifle like a yoke-pin, he should declare that about him among them, saying, 'this is the king's power.'

Old thieves, cow-herds, fowlers and hunters, winning the confidence of forest thieves and foresters, should induce them to attack caravans, herds or villages with plenty of articles made of artificial gold and forest produce.

When the attack is made, they should get them killed by stupefying liquids.

Or, they should get the criminals arrested while sleeping after being tired by a long journey carrying a heavy load of stolen goods or when they are intoxicated by drugged liquor at festive parties.

And after they have been caught, the administrator should show them as before to the people, causing a proclamation of the king's omniscience to be made among the inhabitants of the kingdom.

viii) Degree of punishment of criminals

The king shall not put to torture a person whose offence is trifling, or who is a minor or aged or sick or intoxicated or insane or overcome by hunger, thirst or travel, or who has overeaten or whose meal is undigested or who is weak. He should cause them to be secretly watched by persons of the same character, prostitutes, attendants at water-booths and givers of advice, accommodation and food to them.

References

Ballantyne, James R. (translator) (1885): Sankhya Aphorisms of Kapila, London, Trubner & Co., Ludgate Hill.

Devi Purana (Devi Bhagavatam)

Sanskrit: 1. Shrimad devi Bhagavat MahaPuran, Sanskrit Text with Hindi Translation, 2016 Edition, Gorakhpur, Gita Press.

[https://ia801307.us.archive.org/9/items/
SrimadDeviBhagavatamSanskrit/
Srimad%20Devi%20Bhagavatam%20-%20Sanskrit.pdf]
   English: [http://upload.vedpuran.net/Uploads/
68655SrimadDeviPurana.pdf]

Chapter-2: Espionage in Arthaśāstra - External

This chapter takes into account the following sub-topics:

Foreign Policy and Circle of Kings

Foreign policy of the protagonist king as envisaged by Kauṭilya is an aggressive one, to subjugate the other states in the circle of states in order to unify the entire Indian subcontinent into a vast state under the protagonist king (vijigīṣu or chakravartin). Therefore, the primary objective of Kauṭilya's External Espionage was to assist invasion and subjugation by the protagonist king of the other sovereign states (tribal republics, oligarchies, petty monarchies etc.) by war efforts and deceit. To understand the situation in the Indian subcontinent at Kauṭily's time let us have a glimpse of the theory pertaining to maṇḍala (circle of states).

Kauṭilya's external espionage is inexorably associated with the theory pertaining to the circle of states. The political objective of the Kauṭilya's king was to subjugate all the states in the circle and his espionage network had a crucial role in the success of the king in this regard.

The protagonist king is conceived as governing a state in a circle (maṇḍala) surrounded by other states which are either friendly, or inimical or neutral vis-à-vis the protagonist king's state.

The maṇḍala theory is not any novel invention of Kauṭilya. There are mentions of 'circle of states' and of chakravartin ruling the entire Indian subcontinent or even the entire world in Maitrayaniya Upaniṣada, Hindu Mythologies, Mahābhārata and Buddhist texts. However, Kauṭilya, for the first time, delineated concrete steps towards formation of a large state by subjugating the other constituents of the circle of states by the chakravartin.

Kauṭilya considers the would-be conqueror (vijigīṣu or chakravartin) to be a part of a maṇḍala or circle of kings or states. There are friends, enemies, neutral states and intermediary or middle states around the protagonist, the would-be conqueror. Kauṭilya considers the state immediately outside the border to be an enemy and the state immediately after this enemy, the ally.

The king of the state with territory immediately proximate to those of the enemy and the conqueror is called the middle king. The king of the state outside the sphere of the enemy, the conqueror and the middle king, stronger than their constituents, capable of helping the enemy, the conqueror and the middle king when they are united and of suppressing them when they are disunited, is defined by Kauṭilya as the neutral king.

Now the circle can be expanded further including enemy's friend and foe; ally's friend and foe; intermediate state's friend and foe, and neutral state's friend and foe and so on.

Kauṭilya describes vividly how by open warfare, devious means, deceptive warfare etc., the would-be conqueror could subjugate the other states in the circle and become the sole ruler of the entire circle of states. Espionage mechanism is to play a crucial role in this regard.

Four Methods to Conquer the World

The conquering process by the vijigīṣu ought to be gradual and Kauṭilya mentions four methods of subjugating the entire circle, each method applicable for a specific objective condition i.e., the relative position of various types of kings vis-à-vis the protagonist in the circle.

The four methods to conquer the world (actually the entire Indian subcontinent) are as follows:

i) First Method

At first, the vijigīṣu king should conquer the territory of the immediate enemy state by fair means or foul. After conquering the enemy's territory, he should seek to seize the territory of the middle king, and after subjugating the latter his endeavour would be to subjugate the neutral king.

According to Kauṭilya, this is the first method of conquering the entire maṇḍala.

ii) Second Method

In case of nonexistence of middle and neutral kings, the vijigīṣu ought to subjugate the enemy king by means of superior policy, open or deceitful. This, according to Kauṭilya, is the second method of conquering the world.

iii) Third Method

In the absence of the circle, the protagonist should overcome by squeezing from both sides the ally through the enemy or the enemy through the ally. This is the third method of conquering according to Kauṭilya.

iv) Fourth Method

The fourth method as prescribed by Kauṭilya is that the vijigīṣu king should first overcome a weak or a single neighbouring king. So he would now become doubly powerful, and with this combined power he should proceed to subjugate a second king who is a little more powerful than the weakest king subjugated at first. Then with the combined power of the three the vijigīṣu king should tackle a third king and the process would continue until the entire circle of states is under the control of the vijigīṣu.

Now let us see how Kauṭilya's External Espionage methods are to be administered to make the above objective fulfilled. In this chapter we take up the general espionage to accomplish the target and we are going to take up espionage related to war efforts in the next chapter.

Setting up Spy Network in the Maṇḍala

The king should plant spies among high officials and all other establishments of the enemy, the ally, the middle king, and the neutral king.

Humpbacks, dwarfs, eunuchs, women skilled in arts, dumb person and different types of mleccha races (non-Aryan outcastes) should be employed as spies living inside the houses of the officials of enemy and other kings.

In fortified towns traders should constitute the spy establishments; on the outskirts of fortified towns, ascetics; farmers and apostate monks in the countryside, and herdsmen on the borders of the country.

In the forest should be placed forest-dwellers such as monks, foresters and others – a series of spies, quick in their work – in order to gather information about activities of the enemy king and other kings.

All Embracing Spy-Network in the Maṇḍala

In the entire circle, the protagonist king should station envoys and secret agents everywhere, in all establishments and offices of all other kings in the maṇḍala.

All sorts of provocations, deceits, bribing and secret assassinations through poisoning and other measures are to be undertaken by the spies under various guises to generate disputes, chaos and confusion in the states of the other kings which could be conducive for the protagonist to have gradual command over the other kings.

Double agents

Spies of all categories should live with enemies receiving wages from them, in order to find out secret information, without associating with one another. They would play the roles of double agents i.e., persons in the pay of both.

The protagonist king should appoint such double agents after taking charge of their sons and wives. The king should ascertain their loyalty through other spies of their type. The captivity of the kinsmen by the protagonist king would ensure the actual loyalty of the double agents to the protagonist only.

Winning the Seducible in the Enemy Camp

The persons in the enemy side who could be seduced according to Kauṭilya belong mainly to the following categories: Enraged, Frightened, Greedy and Proud.

Among them the protagonist should cause instigation through spies appearing as holy men with shaven heads or matted hair – of each person of the seducible party by that spy to whom he may be devoted. He should win over the seducible in the enemy's territories by means of conciliation and gifts and those not seducible by means of dissension and force, pointing out to them the defects of the enemy.

i) For the enraged

The spies are to instigate those in the enemy side who are enraged against his own king and add fuel to their anger by comparing their king as an intoxicated elephant destroying the citizens and their properties. If they are convinced of this, the spies would suggest them to erect a rival elephant to contain and destroy the mad king. In this way the spies would initiate an uprising of the enraged against the enemy king.

ii) For the frightened

The spies should instigate the citizens who are frightened of their own king of the enemy country by comparing the enemy king with a poisonous serpent and insist that to save themselves from the venom of the serpent like king they should leave their country and take shelter of a benevolent king (the protagonist).

iii) For the greedy

To instigate the greedy persons, the spy should make statements that their king favours only those who are devoid of spirit, intelligence and eloquence, but fails to appreciate and do favour to them although they possess praiseworthy qualities. Once they are convinced, the spies should suggest that if they abandon their own king and join hands with the protagonist king, they would be highly benefited as the other (protagonist) king knows how to appreciate and reward persons of distinction.

iv) For the proud

To instigate the proud, the spy should make statements like, 'Just as the well of the candalas is of use only to the candalas, not to others, so this king, being low, is of benefit only to low persons, not to Aryas such as you; that other king (the protagonist) knows how to appreciate persons of distinction; go to him.'

When they have been instigated to go against his own king and desire to be ally of the protagonist, they should be employed according to their capacity in his own works, with spies to watch over them.

v) For Other seducible persons

Secret agents working in close proximity to the enemy king and the king's favorites should gain confidence of those in the position of friends to chiefs of infantry, cavalry, chariots and elephants and inform that the king is enraged with them.

When the rumors have become widespread, assassins should go to their houses and inform them that the king had ordered them to come with the spies.

As soon as they come out, the assassin-spies should kill them and announce audibly to the persons in the vicinity that they have done this by order of their king. And to those who have not been slain, secret agents should say that they too would face the same fate and he who wants to remain alive should go away.

To those to whom the king does not give something when asked for it, secret agents should instigate them against their king by saying that they are under suspicion of the king who is likely to punish them with death sentence. So, they should go away and join the protagonist in order to evade death sentence.

To those who do not ask the enemy king for something that ought to be asked for, secret agents should say that the Regent was told by the king, 'such and such persons do not ask me for something which ought to be asked for; this must be because they are apprehensive of their own guilt? Strive to exterminate them.' Then they should act as before.

Deceptive Peace Treaty and its Violation

Son pledged in peace treaty

If the king is in a difficult situation and forced to make a treaty with the stronger enemy, he may pledge his son as guarantee and come out of the existing trouble through surrender and peace treaty. Once in a safe and strong position, the spies are to take out his son from captivity by trickery and thereafter he may violate the treaty.

The methods suggested in Arthaśāstra for taking out the king's pledged son from captivity are:

Secret agents disguised as traders should administer poison to guards by selling cooked food and fruits. Or, secret agents disguised as gallants, minstrels, physicians or vendors of cooked food should set fire at night to the houses of the rich or of the guards.

Under the chaos and confusion created by spies in the above manner, the captive prince should be made to appear as a corpse and carried out by secret agents.

Other agents disguised as foresters should misguide the direct pursuers to the opposite direction to which the rescuer of the prince are fleeing.

Or, taking up weapons secretly brought, and falling on the guards at night, the prince should escape on quick-marching horses along with secret agents.

Creating Dissentions in the Circle of Kings

i) In the circle of kings when a friendly king declines to come to terms with the protagonist, deceitful means should be resorted to in order to win him over. The spies should adopt various underhand means to separate this friendly king from the enemy and win him over.

ii) The first and foremost endeavour should be to win over the last among combined friends, because, Kauṭilya emphasizes that when friendship with him is secured, those who occupy the middle rank will be separated from each other.

iii) The protagonist should attempt through spies to win over a friend who occupies the middle rank. Kauṭilya explains that if friendship with a king occupying the middle rank in the circle of kings is ensured, friends, occupying the extreme ranks cannot keep the union of the maṇḍala. In brief, according to Kauṭilya, all conceivable measures that tend to break the combination of kings in the circle should be employed by the protagonist.

iv) If any two of the kings in the circle are apprehensive of enmity and seizure of land from each other, spies should be deployed to sow seeds of dissension between them. The timid of the two may be made suspicious about the other through the spies who would insist that the other would take advantage of the peace treaty between them to destroy him. So he should break the peace treaty at once and join hands with the protagonist.

v) When from one's own country or from another's country commodities should arrive for entry in the warehouse in the enemy country, spies of the protagonist should spread the rumour that those commodities have been received from one whom the enemy wanted to march against. When the report is spread wide, the protagonist should send a false writ with a man condemned to death, 'These goods have been sent by me to you as a present; attack your confederates or desert them; then you will receive the rest of the stipulated amount.'

Then spies of the protagonist should inform the other kings in the maṇḍala, 'These articles are given to him by your enemy.' And in this manner they could sow the seeds of mistrust and discord among the kings in the maṇḍala.

vi) The protagonist should collect some merchandise peculiar to the country of one of his enemies and unknown elsewhere. Secret agents disguised as merchants, would sell that merchandise to other enemies and tell them that that merchandise was given to the protagonist by the enemy whose country's product it is. This would lead to distrust and discord between the enemy to whose country the product belongs and the other enemies to whom the product is sold by the spies of the protagonist.

vii) The protagonist through the network of spies should purchase with wealth and honour those who are highly treacherous among an enemy's people and direct them to live with the enemy, armed with weapons, poison and fire. Then one of the ministers of the enemy may be killed by these miscreants. The sons and wife of the assassinated minister should be induced to say that the minister was killed at night by such and such a person. Then another minister of the enemy may be induced to ask every one of the family of the murdered minister about the cause of the death.

If they say in reply as they are taught by the spies, they may be caused to be set free; if they do not do so, they may be caused to be caught hold of.

viii) Spies after gaining the confidence of the enemy king should tell him that he has to guard himself from such and such a minister. Then the double agents receiving salaries from both the protagonist and the enemy should induce the suspected minister to kill his king.

ix) Kings in the maṇḍala possessing enthusiasm and power may be instigated by the spies of the protagonist to seize the kingdom of a particular king in the maṇḍala. Then these secret agents of the protagonist should inform the particular king of the attempt of the other kings to capture his kingdom. Thereafter secret agents should destroy the camp or supplies or allied troops of one of the other kings in the maṇḍala and pass the blame on to the particular king. Other spies, pretending to be friends, should inform these kings that they should destroy the particular king.

Stirring up the Circle of Kings

Kauṭilya suggests the following deceitful measures by the protagonist to stir up the kings belonging to the maṇḍala.

i) A spy after gaining trust of the enemy king should cause latter to understand that some of his high officers is in communication with men of the enemy. As a proof of this, the spy should show other spies posing as treasonable men carrying letters from the enemy for the suspected officers.

ii) After tempting with land or money the principal officers among the chiefs of the army of the enemy, the spy appointed for this purpose by the protagonist should make them fight their own people or he should carry these officers of the enemy away.

iii) Spies should instigate that son of the enemy king who is not in favour of the king that the prince who has been favoured and selected to be crowned as the successor suspects him and has plotting to kill him. So, for his own safety and rightful claim of the throne, he should fight and kill the crown prince and the king with the help of the protagonist.

iv) After luring with money a disgruntled member of the family of the enemy king or a prince in disfavour, the spy of the protagonist should instigate him to crush the troops of the enemy king with assistance from the protagonist.

v) After winning the wild tribes with money and honour, the spies should utilize them to destroy the kingdom of the enemy king.

vi) The protagonist should say to the enemy in the rear of the enemy, 'This king, after exterminating me, will indeed exterminate you; attack him in the rear; if he turns round on you, I shall attack him to the rear.'

vii) The protagonist should say to the allies of the enemy, 'I am your dam; with me broken, this king will overwhelm all of you; let us join together and frustrate his expedition.'

viii) The protagonist should send letters in connection with his enemy to those united with him and to those not united with this mission, 'This king, after uprooting me, will indeed take action against you; beware; it is better for you to help me.'

ix) The protagonist should send appeals to the middle king or again to the neutral king, according as the one or the other may be near, making a surrender to him of all possessions, in order to be saved.

x) Spies should dispose of a fiery or energetic enemy or one in a calamity or one entrenched in a fort, by weapon, fire, poison and so on, or one of them should do so because of ease in doing it.

For, an assassin, single-handed, may be able to achieve his end with weapon, poison and fire.

xi) If any one of the kings in the maṇḍala has fear of or enmity towards or hatred of another, spies of the protagonist should divide him from the other, suggesting, 'This king is making peace with your enemy; presently he will overreach you; make peace yourself very quickly and try to restrain him.'

Thereafter, guilds of castes, supported by one another, should strike at their weak points, and secret agents should strike with fire, poison and weapon.

Sowing Dissensions among Tribal Republics and Oligarchies

According to Kauṭilya, the single monarch should deal with oligarchies and tribal republics in the following manner.

i) Spies of the protagonist close to the members of oligarchies or tribal republics should find out one another's defects, and occasions for mutual hatred, enmity or strife among members of the oligarchy, and should sow discord in one who is gradually brought round to believe them, saying, 'So and so is slandering you.'

When resentment is thus built up on both the sides, agents serving as teachers should start quarrels among pupils concerning learning, skill, gambling and pleasure sports.

ii) Spies should instigate quarrels among the followers of the chiefs in the oligarchy by praising the opponents in brothels and taverns, or by supporting seducible parties.

iii) Spies should stir up very young princes enjoying low comforts with a longing for superior comforts.

iv) Spies should prevent inter-dining or inter-marrying of the superior with the inferior.

Or, they should urge inferiors to inter-dining or inter-marrying with superiors.

Or, they should urge the very low ones to obtain a position of equality in the matter of family, valor or change of status.

Or, they should nullify a transaction that is settled by establishing its opposite.

v) In cases of legal disputes, assassins should start quarrels by injuring objects, cattle or men at night.

In all cases of strife, the protagonist should support the weak party with treasury and troops and urge them to kill the rival party.

vi) At the time of fighting, spies appearing as wine sellers should offer, in hundreds, jars of wine mixed with a stupefying liquid, as libation to the deceased, under the pretext of the death of a son or wife.

vii) Spies should point out the depositing of an object after an agreement, such as sealed bags with money and vessels containing money, at the gates of sanctuaries or temples and near fortified places.

When members of the oligarchy are seen approaching, they should declare, 'These belong to the king.'

Then the spies should make an attack.

viii) Or, a secret agent should say to a son of a chief of the ruling council, who thinks highly of himself, 'You are the son of such and such a king, kept here through fear of the enemy.'

When the proud prince is instigated by the praise of the spy, the protagonist should support him with treasury and troops and make him fight the members of the oligarchy. When the design of the protagonist through the vainglorious prince is fulfilled, the prince should be killed by the assassins appointed for that purpose.

ix) Keepers of prostitutes, acrobats, actors, dancers or showmen, employed as agents, should make chiefs of the ruling council infatuated with women possessed of great beauty and youth.

When passion is roused in them, they should be made by deceitful means to get involved in quarrel over the women. During the quarrel, assassins should slay them.

x) Or, if anyone of the frustrated chiefs puts up with his disappointment, the whore involved should instigate him to murder another chief by saying, 'Such and such a chief is harassing me, because I am in love with you; so long as he is alive, I cannot stay with you. So, kill him to get me.'

xi) Or, the woman, if forcibly abducted, should get the abductor murdered at night by assassins at the edge of the park or in a pleasure house, or should herself kill him with poison.

Then she should proclaim, 'My lover has been killed by so and so.'

xii) Or, an agent appearing as a holy man should create confidence in a chief, in whom passion is roused, by means of love-winning herbs and then killing him with poison he should disappear.

When he has gone away, secret agents should declare that it is the act of another chief.

xiii) Female secret agents posing as rich widows or living by a secret profession, and contending for inheritance or a deposit should infatuate chiefs of the ruling council.

When they have agreed and come to secret houses for the night's meeting with the woman, assassins should kill them or imprison them.

xiv) Or, a secret agent should describe to a chief of the oligarchy who is fond of women, 'In such and such a village, the family of a poor man has migrated; his wife is fit for a king; seize her.'

When she is seized, after a fortnight, an agent appearing as a holy man should cry out in the midst of the chiefs of the treasonable oligarchy, 'That chief has violated my wife or daughter-in-law or sister or daughter.'

If the ruling council were to chastise the chief, the protagonist should support the condemned chief and make him fight against those hostile to him.

If he is not punished, assassins should slay at night the agent appearing as a holy man.

Then others appearing in the same disguise should cry out, 'so and so is a Brāhmaṇa-slayer and the paramour of a Brāhmaṇa woman.'

xv) An agent appearing as an astrologer, should describe a maiden chosen as the bride by one chief to another, 'the daughter or so and so is destined to become the wife of a king or the mother of a king; get her by spending all you have or by force.'

If she cannot be obtained, he should rouse the other party.

If she is obtained, the strife is at once brought about.

xvi) Or, a female mendicant should say to a chief fond of his wife, 'Such and such a chief, conceited by reason of youth, sent me to your wife; through fear of him I have brought a letter and ornaments from him; your wife is innocent; steps against him should be taken secretly; in the meantime I shall accept on your wife's behalf.'

On these and other occasions of strife, whether the strife has arisen of its own accord or has been created by assassins, the king should support the weak party with treasury and troops and make him fight against those hostile to him.

Counter Espionage

Along with offensive espionage network against the enemies the protagonist should also take appropriate measures to guard his country against espionage networks of the enemies. So, along with offensive espionage, Kauṭilya emphasizes the necessity of building up counter-espionage network by the protagonist. The protagonist should undertake the following measures to ensure security against espionage of the enemy.

All types of spies deployed by the enemy against the protagonist or spy networks of the enemy should be detected by similar categories of his own spies and spy establishments.

In order to discover espionage by enemies, he should station at frontiers principal officers, who are non-seducible, but are enlightened with the method to learn from the seducible of the enemy side about the espionage scheme of the enemy.

Immaculate vigilance should be undertaken even during by day-time in order to discover spying by the enemy.

Chapter-1: Espionage in Arthaśāstra – War Related

Introduction

Success in war depends a good deal on espionage mechanism. It is very difficult for any country to be successful in war without an advanced network of external espionage. In modern world it is found that espionage plays a very important role in war, for example, in the two World Wars. A glaring example of the role of espionage to enable a country to win a war is the role of the super-spy Eli Cohen in the six-day Israel-Arab War of 1967.

The super spy Eli Cohen was planted in Syria by the Israeli intelligence agency Mossad under the guise of an Arab trader. Cohen was considered as the right person for the mission as he looked exactly like an Arab.

Only because of him Israel could achieve such great success in the 6 day war with Arab countries in 1967, especially it was intelligence provided by Eli that enabled Israel to capture so easily Golan heights, the almost invincible defense line of Syria. (Lazo, 2019).

Now let us pass on to the guidelines delineated in Arthaśāstra pertaining to use of espionage mechanism in war.

The major aspects of war related espionage mechanism as depicted in Arthaśāstra are:

Instilling Superstitious Fear in the Enemy Camp

Assassination of the Enemy's Army Chiefs

Destruction of Enemy Supplies and Reinforcements

Killing the Enemy King by Deceit

Overreaching the Enemy with Trickery

Capturing the Enemy's Fort

Drawing Out the Enemy King by Tricks

Entering Enemy's Fort by Stratagem

Seizure and Storming of Enemy's Fort

Pacification of the Conquered Territory

Instilling Superstitious Fear in the Enemy Camp

Spies under the guise of astrologers and others should fill the side of the king with enthusiasm by proclaiming omniscience of the protagonist king and association with divine agencies. On the other hand, they should fill the enemy's side with terror.

The various means as suggested by Kauṭilya to strike terror among the soldiers and citizens of the enemy side include: occult practices, deployment of assassins for slaying people belonging to the enemy camp, deceiving the enemy by magical arts, a show of association with divinities, frightening with elephants, rousing the treasonable in the enemy side, setting fire to camps, attacks on the tips and the rear of the enemy, creating dissensions in the enemy side through agents appearing as messengers saying, 'your fort has been burnt down or captured; a revolt by a member of your family has broken out'; or, 'your enemy or a forest chieftain has risen against you.'

As regards the power of espionage mechanism Kauṭilya emphasizes that an arrow, discharged by an archer, may kill one person or may not kill even one; but espionage activities operated by an expert spy would kill even children in the womb.

Assassination of the Enemy's Army Chiefs

i) Exploiting the vice of lust

Keepers of prostitutes under the protagonist should make the enemy's army chiefs infatuated with women possessed of great beauty and youth. When many or two of the chiefs feel passion for one woman, assassins should create quarrels among them.

Agents should urge the party who is defeated in the strife to go away elsewhere or to render help to the protagonist in the expedition against the enemy.

Or, spies under the guise of ascetics would administer poison to those among the chiefs who have been infatuated by the harlots by saying that this (the poison) is the drug to win love of women.

Or, an agent appearing as a trader should shower wealth on an intimate maid of the favourite queen of the enemy for the sake of love and then leave her. An agent appearing as a holy man, recommended by an agent appearing as an attendant of the same trader, should give a love-winning medicine to the maid to administer it on the trader to win back his love. As prearranged the trader would once again start favouring the maid. On the basis of the success of this medicine, the spy posing as assistant to the trader should advise the maid to inform the efficacy of the remedy to win love and so the queen should use this to win the love and favour of the king. If the queen agrees to do so, the spy would replace the earlier remedy with poison.

ii) Exploiting the vice of pride

An agent appearing as an astrologer should declare to the prime minister of the enemy, whose confidence has been gradually won, that he is possessed of the marks of a king. At the same time a spy under the guise of a female mendicant should tell the minister's wife that she has the characteristics of a queen and that she would give birth to a prince.

Or, a female agent disguised as a minister's wife, complain to the prime minister of the enemy that their king has been attempting to keep her in his harem. She would show a letter and ornaments and declare that these have been sent to her by the king through a female mendicant in order to tempt her.

Or, an agent appearing as a cook or a waiter should inform a chief about the king's instruction for administering poison to him and the money offered to tempt him to do so.

An agent appearing as a trader should corroborate that information of his, and should speak of the success of the undertaking.

In this manner, with one, two or three means, the protagonist through spies should incite the high officers one by one to fight or to desert the enemy king.

iii) Through rumours

In fortified cities of the enemy king, secret agents serving in close proximity to the resident governor, should declare among citizens and country people, as if out of friendship, that the governor has said to warriors and heads of departments, 'the king is in a difficult position; he may or may not come back alive; obtain wealth by force and slay your enemies.'

When the rumor has spread far and wide, assassins should rob citizens at night and slay chiefs, saying at the time, 'thus are dealt with those who do not obey the governor.'

Thereafter, they should leave blood-stained weapons, articles and binding ropes in the quarters of the governor.

Then secret agents should proclaim, 'the governor is slaying and robbing the subjects.'

In the same manner, they should divide the country people from collector general of the country.

Assassins should kill the subordinates of the collector general in the midst of villages at night and say, 'thus are dealt with those who oppress the countryside unrighteously.'

Spreading the false news of the danger of the enemy, the spies may set fire to the harem, the gates of the town and the store-house of grains and other things, and slay the sentinels who are kept to guard them and pass the blame to the governor and the collector general.

When trouble has thus started, the spies should cause the governor and the collector general to be killed by an uprising of the subjects. Thereafter, the spies should get clansmen of the person killed installed in the place of assassinated officials.

Destruction of Enemy Supplies and Reinforcements

a) The protagonist's secret agents who are living disguised as traders in the fortified towns of the enemy, disguised as householders in his villages, disguised as cow-herds and ascetics in the frontier posts of the enemy's country, should send, along with presents word to a neighbouring prince, a forest chief, a disgruntled or greedy member of the enemy's clan or a prince of the enemy kingdom in disfavour that the enemy's country is to be captured. And when secret emissaries come as invited, the spies of the protagonist should welcome them with money and honour and show them the weak points of the enemy. Thereafter the spies should undertake combined attack on these weak points of the enemy kingdom.

b) An agent appearing as a wine-seller in the enemy's camp, establishing a person condemned to death as his son and killing him by poison at the time of an attack should offer, in hundreds, jars of wine as libation in honour of the dead. He should give on the first day unadulterated wine or wine with one quarter poison, and later on give wine mixed wholly with poison.

c) Giving unadulterated wine to the army chiefs of the enemy, the spy of the protagonist under the guise of a wine-seller should give them wine mixed with poison when they are in a state of intoxication.

d) An agent, under the guise of a chief officer of the enemy's army, may adopt the same measures as those employed by the seller of wine.

e) Spies of the protagonist, disguised as dealers in cooked meat, cooked rice, liquor or cakes, should advertise their special goods and, may vie with each other in proclaiming in public the sale of a fresh supply of their special articles at cheap price and may sell the articles mixed with poison to the attracted customers of the enemy.

f) Spies under the guise of women and children, purchasing wine, milk, curds, butter or oil from spies as dealers in these commodities, should pour them in their own vessels containing poison. After mixing with poison they should pour them back to in the vessels of the seller saying, 'give us something else at this price, or give us of better quality again.' Agents appearing as traders or those who bring goods for sale to the camp should sell these poison-mixed articles to the genuine buyers of the enemy camp.

g) Spies in the guise of merchants should give their goods to the spies (under various guises) staying near the horses and elephants and these spies in their turn should mix poison into fodder and grass for the elephants and the horses. Or, spies appearing as workmen should sell grass or water mixed with poison.

h) Spies disguised as cattle traders, having long association with the enemy camp, should let lose their own herds of cattle or of sheep and goats on the occasion of an attack, in places likely to cause confusion among the enemies, and also should let loose the vicious among horses, donkeys, camels, buffaloes and other animals. Or, agents appearing as above should let loose animals whose eyes have been smeared with the blood of musk-rats.

i) Spies appearing as hunters should let loose wild animals from their cages, or snake charmers, serpents with deadly poison, or those living by elephants, elephants.

j) Spies living by fire should set fire to things.

k) Secret agents should kill from behind the chiefs of infantry, cavalry, chariots or elephants when they have turned back, or should set fire to the quarters of the chiefs.

l) Traitors, wild tribes, forest troops employed by the protagonist should attack and destroy the enemy's rear or obstruct his reinforcements.

m) Spies concealed in forests should lure out troops on the frontier and slay them, or should destroy the supplies, the reinforcements and foraging raids on a path passable by a single man only.

Killing the Enemy King by Deceit

i) In course of a night-battle the spies should announce through coded loud striking of drums, 'we have entered it; the kingdom is won.' And entering the king's quarters, they should kill the king in the tumult.

ii) If the enemy king tries to escape, leaders of mleccha and forest troops, on all sides, taking cover in places of ambush or taking cover behind hedges of tree-stems, should kill him.

iii) Or, secret agents appearing as hunters should, in the tumult of an attack, strike at the enemy king on occasions fit for secret fights. Or, they should strike at him when he is on a path where marching in a single file alone is possible or on a mountain, or behind a hedge of tree-stems or in a marshy place or inside water, in accordance with the suitability of the terrain to the spies themselves.

iv) Or, the spies should drown the enemy king through a rush of water by breaking dams in rivers, lakes and tanks.

v) Or, if the enemy king is in a desert fort, a forest fort or a water fort, spies of the protagonist should destroy him with poisonous fire and smoke.

vi) Assassins should do away with the enemy king by fire when he is in a narrow place, by smoke when he is in a desert, by poison if he is in his residence, by frightful crocodiles or persons moving in water if he has taken a plunge in water, or kill him as he is coming out of his quarters set on fire.

Overreaching the Enemy with Trickery

When the protagonist is confronted with an enemy likely to be more powerful than him and apprehends the possibility of his fort being under the siege by the powerful enemy, Kauṭilya insists that the protagonist should first take measures to put difficulty on the path of advance of the enemy, and make all conceivable endeavours to ensure his own security.

The measures prescribed by Kauṭilya under such a difficult situation may be summarized in the following manner.

Precautionary measures

i) The protagonist should cause grass and wood to be burnt up to one yojana on all sides of his fort. Water should be vitiated and caused to flow away; and he should place wells, concealed pits and barbed wires outside.

ii) Making an underground with many openings up to the enemy's camp, the protagonist should cause the chiefs of stores of the enemy to be carried away, or the enemy himself may also be likewise carried off.

iii) If an underground passage is made by the enemy for his own use, the protagonist should cause the moat outside the fort to be dug deeper till its water reaches the underground passage of the enemy.

iv) In suspected places along the parapet of the enemy's fort and in the house containing a well outside the fort, he should place jars of water in order to find out the direction of the wind blowing from the underground tunnel of the enemy. When the direction of the tunnel is found out, he should cause a counter passage to be dug. Or, breaking it in the middle, he should let in smoke or water.

v) Appointing a kinsman for the defence of the fort, the protagonist should move in the opposite direction of that of the enemy, or where he might be united with allies, kinsmen or forest chiefs or with great enemies and traitors of the enemy, or to such a place from where the protagonist can separate the enemy from his allies or from where he may strike at the enemy's rear, or country, or from where he may prevent the transport of supplies to his enemy, or whence he may strike his enemy by throwing down trees at hand, or from where he can find means to defend his own country or is capable of causing reinforcements of his army; or he may go to any other country from where he can obtain peace on his own terms.

vi) Those who have left the fort of the protagonist with him should send a mission to the enemy, 'This enemy of yours has fallen in our hands; on the pretext of the purchase of a commodity or of doing injury, send money and a strong force, to which we should hand him over, bound or killed.'

If the enemy king agrees to the proposal and sends money and army as asked for, the protagonist should appropriate the money and the force deployed by the enemy king.

vii) Or, the commander in charge of a frontier fort of the protagonist, by pretending to surrender the fort, should get a part of the enemy's troops inside and destroy them when they are in full trust of the pretender.

viii) The administrator of the fort of the protagonist, pretending to aid the enemy, should invite a division of the enemy's army to destroy the country people stationed in one place. When it is led by spies to an enclosed region, the administrator should destroy it when full of trust.

ix) When a fort of the protagonist is under siege, a secret agent of the protagonist posing as a friend of the besieger should send a message to him, 'In this fort. Grains, fats, sugar or salt is exhausted; new stocks of it will come in at this place and time; seize it.'

Then traitors, wild tribes and other enemies of the besieger should bring in poisoned grains, fats, sugar or salt. Convicts condemned to death may also be appointed to bring these poisoned articles. The enemy is likely to be tempted to seize these poisoned articles by force and thereafter be in trouble.

x) Having made peace with the conqueror, the protagonist may give the conqueror part of the ransom promised and assure him of paying the rest by installments. Then he should wait for conqueror's (enemy's) defensive force to be slackened and then strike them down with fire, poison or sword; or he may win the confidence of the conqueror's courtiers deputed to take the tribute.

xi) If the resources of the protagonist are exhausted, he may flee from his fort. Abandoning his fort, the protagonist should escape through a tunnel or through a hole made into the parapet.

xii) Having challenged the conqueror at night, the protagonist should try to confront the attack of the enemy. If he fails to do so, he may escape through a side path disguised as a heretic. Or he may be carried out by spies decked as a corpse; or he may escape under the guise of a woman following the corpse of her dead husband (arranged by spies).

xiii) When the enemy is preoccupied with festivities in a pleasure park or other recreation grounds, assassins, entering through underground chambers or tunnels or hollow walls, should slay him, or those employed in secret service should do so by poison.

xiv) When the enemy king is sleeping in a secluded place, female secret agents should drop on him serpents or poisonous fire or smoke. Calling by signals or drums, door-keepers, eunuchs and others secretly employed with the enemy, he should get the rest of the enemies killed.

xv) Secret agents should introduce weapons in the articles for the enemy king's sports and in objects from the stores used by him. And agents following a secret activity, moving about at night, and those living by fire, should put fire in those objects.

Capturing the Enemy's Fort

(i) Through magic and occult practices

The would be conqueror, desirous of seizing the enemy's fortified town, should infuse his own side with enthusiasm and frighten the enemy's side by giving publicity to the power of omniscience and close association with gods of the protagonist.

The proclamation of his omniscience is to be made in the following manner: rejection of his chief officers after ascertaining their secret, domestic and other private affairs through spies; disclosing the names of traitors after receiving information from spies specially employed to find out such men and proclaiming that the king has known them by means of his power of omniscience; pretensions to the knowledge of foreign affairs by means of the power of the protagonist to read omens and signs invisible to others when information about foreign affairs is just received through a domestic pigeon which has brought a sealed letter.

The proclamation of association with divinities, however, should be arranged thus: conversing with and worshipping agents appearing as deities in fire-sanctuaries, who have entered the hollow images of deities in fire-sanctuaries by an underground passage; or, conversing with and worshipping agents appearing as Nagas or Varuna [1] risen from the water; placing under water at night a mass of sea-foam mixed with burning oil, and exhibiting it as the spontaneous outbreak of fire, when it is burning in a line; sitting on a raft in water which is secretly fastened by a rope to a rock; such magical performance in water as is usually done at night by bands of magicians, using the sack of abdomen or womb of water animals to hide the head and the nose, and applying to the nose the oil, prepared from the entrails of red spotted deer and the serum of the flesh of the crab, crocodile, porpoise and otter; holding conversation, as though, with women of Varuna (the god of water), or of Naga (the snake-god) when they are performing magical tricks in water; and sending out volumes of smoke from the mouth on occasions of anger.

Soothsayers, interpreters of omens, astrologers, persons reciting Puranas, seers, and secret agents, those who have helped and those who have witnessed it, should give wide publicity to that power of the protagonist king to associate with gods throughout his territory.

In the enemy's territory, they should speak about the protagonist king's meeting with divinities and the acquisition of a treasury and army from a divine source.

And when interpreting questions to deities, omens, crow's flight, the science of the body, dreams and utterances of animals and birds, they should predict victory for the protagonist, and defeat for the enemy. And they should point to a meteor in the enemy's constellation with a beat of drum.

(ii) Through secret agents

Agents working as envoys, speaking to the chiefs of the enemy out of friendship, should tell them of the king's high regard for them, of the strengthening of his own party and the deterioration of the enemy's party.

The secret agents under the guise of chief messengers of the protagonist, pretending to be friendly towards the enemy, should highly speak of the protagonist's respectful treatment of visitors, of the strength of his army capable of bringing about destruction of his enemy's men. The spies should also make it known to the enemy that under their master, both ministers and soldiers are equally safe and happy, and that their master treats his servants with parental care in their weal and woe.

By these and other means, they should win over the enemy's men and stir up the enemy's party against the enemy king.

The spies ought to adopt variegated ways to stir up people of various characteristics in the enemy side. They should star up the diligent by speaking of the ordinary donkey; the leaders of the army, by stick and striking of the branch; those frightened, by the ram strayed from the herd; those insulted, by a shower of thunder-bolts; those with hopes frustrated, by the cane bearing no fruit, balls of rice to crows and the cloud created by magic; those receiving the reward of honour, by decoration of a disliked wife by one who hates; those secretly put to test, by the tiger-skin and the death-trap; and as eating a piece of the wood of pilu (a herbal plant), or as churning the milk of a she-camel or a she-donkey (for butter) to those who are rendering to him valuable help.

When the spies are successful in convincing the people of the enemy side about the flaws of their own king and the quality and benevolence of the protagonist, and they are willing to desert the enemy king, they may be sent by the spies to the protagonist king to receive wealth and, honour. Those of the enemy who are in need of money and food should be supplied with an abundance of those things. Those who are not interested to receive such things may be presented with ornaments for their wives and children. And on occasions of famine, or troubles by robbers or forest tribes, secret agents installed in enemy country should stir up urban and rural people of enemy kingdom, and should be instigated that their (enemy) king is not helping them to overcome the crisis and so to seek help from elsewhere. If they agree, help should be provided to them by the protagonist to overcome the effects of the calamity.

Drawing Out the Enemy King by Tricks

(i) Through fake religious men

An ascetic with shaven head or with matted locks, living in a mountain cave, and declaring himself to be four hundred years old, should stay in the vicinity of the city with plenty of disciples with matted locks.

And his disciples, approaching with roots and fruits, should induce the ministers and the king to pay a visit to the holy master.

And, visited by the king, the false ascetic should speak of identification marks of former kings and their countries, adding, 'When every one hundred years of my life are completed, I shall enter fire for the fourth time; you have necessarily to be honoured by me; choose three boons.'

When he agrees, he should say, 'You should stay here with sons and wife for seven nights, after arranging a festival with shows.'

He should attack the enemy king while he is staying there.

Or, an agent appearing as a seer of underground objects, with shaven head or with matted hair, having plenty of disciples with matted hair, should place in an ant-hill a bamboo-strip smeared with goat's blood, after smearing it with gold powder, in order that ants may follow it, or place there a hollow tube of gold.

Then a secret agent should tell the king, 'That holy man knows a flowering treasure-trove.'

Questioned by the king, the agent as holy man should say, 'Yes', and point out that proof, or after placing more money in the earth.

And the fake holy man should say to the enemy king, 'This treasure-trove, guarded by a cobra, can be obtained through worship.'

When the enemy king agrees to worship, the spy should say, 'You should stay here with sons and wife for seven nights, after arranging a festival with shows.'

The spy disguising as holy man should attack the enemy king while he is staying there.

Or, as an agent appearing as a seer of underground objects, with his body enveloped in a burning fire at night, should stay at a desolate place. Other agents say to the king after making him gradually entertain faith in him, 'That holy man is able to secure prosperity.'

When the enemy king visits the fake holy man, the latter should advise the king as in the previous cases and should kill him and his family members accompanying him in the worship suggested by the spy as holy man.

Or, agent appearing as a holy man should tempt the king with magical lores and do as in the previous cases.

Or, an agent appearing as a holy man, finding shelter in the temple of an honoured deity of the country, should, by frequent festivities, win over the chiefs among the constituents and gradually overreach the king.

Or, a secret agent appearing as an ascetic with matted locks, all white, would stay in water, with means of getting away to an underground tunnel or chamber under the bank and other secret agents should tell the king, after gradually making him believe, that the pretending holy man is the water god Varuna or the king of the serpents. And by luring the enemy king the spies would attack and kill him as in the previous cases.

Or, an agent appearing as a man of supernatural power, living close to the border of the country, should induce the enemy king to have a look at his enemy (the protagonist king). When the enemy king the spy should make an effigy and summon the enemy (belonging to the protagonist) by means of signals and cause him to be killed, in a secluded spot.

ii) Through fake traders

Agents appearing as traders, coming with horses for sale, should invite the enemy king to purchase or receive horses as a gift, and kill him while engrossed in inspecting the goods or when mingled with horses, should strike with the horses.

iii) Through magic, miracles and occult practices

Assassins, climbing a sacred tree near the city at night-time and blowing into jars through stalks or reeds, should say indistinctly, 'We shall eat the flesh of the king or the chiefs; let worship be offered to us.'

Agents appearing as interpreters of omens and astrologers should make that utterance of theirs known.

Or, agents appearing as Nagas, with their bodies smeared with burning oil, should, at night-time, pound together iron clubs and pestles in a holy lake or in the middle of a tank and utter in the same way.

Or, agents robed in the skins of bears, giving out fire and smoke from the mouths and having the appearance of rakṣasas (demons), should go three times left-wise round the city and utter in the same way, in the intervals between the cries of dogs and jackals.

Or, making the image of a deity in a sanctuary burn at night with burning oil or with fire covered by a layer of mica, secret agents should utter in the same way.

Other spies should make that known.

Or, with blood of animals the spies should cause an excessive flow of blood from honoured images of deities.

Then others should declare defeat in battle in consequence of the flow of the blood of the deity.

Or, on the nights of the month's junctures, the spies should point out a sanctuary in a prominent part of the cemetery where an agent appearing as a rakṣasa should demand the offering of a human being.

And whoever, calling himself brave or someone else, were to come there to see, others should kill him with iron pestles, so that it would be known that he was killed by the rakṣasa.

Those who have witnessed it and secret agents should report that miracle to the king.

Then agents appearing as interpreters of omens and astrologers should prescribe pacification and expiatory rites adding, 'Otherwise a great disaster will befall the king and the country.'

When the enemy king agrees to the proposal he may be asked to perform in person special sacrifices and offerings with special mantras every night for seven days. Then while doing this, he may be killed.

In order to convince the enemy king, the protagonist may himself undertake the performance of expiatory rites to avert such evils. Then he should employ the tricks against them.

iv) Exploiting the passion for hunting

If the enemy king is fond of elephants, spies under the guise of keepers of elephant forests should tempt the enemy king with an elephant possessed of auspicious marks and when he falls into the trap and agrees to accompany the fake elephant keepers in order to capture the elephant, the spies should take him to a dense forest or a path allowing only one person to march at a time, and kill him, or imprison him in accordance with the mandate of the protagonist king. .

v) Exploiting the ṛpu of kāma (lust)

If the enemy king is fond of wealth or women, he may be lured with rich and beautiful widows brought before him by the spies with a pretended complaint for the recovery of a deposit kept by them in the custody of one of their kinsmen; and when the enemy king comes to meet with such a woman at night as arranged, spies in ambush may kill him with weapons or poison.

vi) In chaos and confusions of religious rites or festivals

On the occasion of the visits of the enemy king to holy men, mendicants, images of deities in sanctuaries and various other religious places, assassins, concealed in underground chambers or passages or inside hollow walls, should strike at him.

The assassin spies should take advantage of the confusion and unguarded condition of the enemy king to strike at him under the following conducive conditions: in those places, in which the king himself is witnessing a dramatic show, or is enjoying himself in a festival or where he is sporting in water; on all occasions of speaking words of reproof and so on, during sacrifices and festive parties, during birth-rites, funeral rites and illnesses, on occasions of love, sorrow or fear; when at a festival of his own people he, being full of trust, careless, or when he moves about without a guard, on a rainy day or in crowds; when he has strayed from the route, or when there is a fire or when he has entered a place without any men in it, assassins, entering with packages of clothes, ornaments and flowers, with beds and seats, or with vessels containing wine and food or with musical instruments, should strike at the enemy along with those employed there beforehand.

The assassin spies should depart after completion of their mission, in the same way as they might have entered on the occasions mentioned above for an ambush to attack the enemy.

Entering Enemy's Fort by Stratagem

The protagonist (aspiring conqueror) may pretend to dismiss a confidential chief of a guild and the dismissed chief should seek shelter with the enemy king. After obtaining shelter with the enemy, he should bring over helpmates and associates from his own country on the pretext of partnership.

With the assistance of a band of secret agents, the sheltered chief should, with the consent of the enemy king, destroy a treasonable town of his master, or an army without elephants and horses but with treasonable principal officers, or a treasonable ally in the rear of his master, and send a mission to the enemy.

He may also seek help from a guild of forest tribes for achieving his goal.

After gaining confidence of the enemy through the above activities the chief should inform his master (the protagonist).

Thereafter the master, under the pretext of an expedition for catching elephants or destruction of forest tribes, should attack the enemy secretly.

After making peace with the enemy, the protagonist should ostensibly dismiss his own confidential ministers. Then they may request the enemy to reconcile them to their master. When the enemy agrees to the request of the dismissed ministers and sends a messenger for this purpose, the conqueror should dismiss the proposal by saying: "Your king is trying to sow the seeds of dissension between me and my ministers."

Thereafter one of the dismissed ministers should go over to the enemy along with a band of spies, disaffected people, traitors, brave thieves, and forest tribes who make no distinction between a friend and a foe. Having secured the trust and good graces of the enemy, the minister should propose to him the destruction of the officers of him (the enemy king), such as the boundary-guard, wild chief, and commander of army, telling the enemy king: "These and other persons are in concert with your enemy." Then these persons may be put to death under the writs of the enemy king.

The protagonist may tell his enemy through spies: "A chief with a powerful army means to offend us both, so let us combine and put him down; you may take possession of his treasury or territory." When the enemy king agrees to the proposal and comes out honoured by the protagonist, he may be killed in a tumult or in an open battle with the chief (in concert with the protagonist).

Secret agents of the protagonist, under the guise of hunters and stationed near the gate of the enemy's fort for selling meat should make friendship with the guards at the gate. Having informed the guards of the approach of robbers or thieves on two or three occasions, they may prove themselves to be of reliable character. Then getting their master's (protagonist's) army stationed in two places, one for destroying a town and the other for a sudden assault, should say to the enemies, 'A band of robbers is close by; there is a great din; let a large force come.'

Handing that over to the troops of their master meant for destroying the town and taking the other troops to the gates of the fort at night, they should say, 'The band of robbers is killed; the troops, successful in the expedition, have come back; open the gate.' Or, those secretly employed there beforehand should open the gates. Along with them they should strike the enemy with the army.

The protagonist should station in the enemy's fort soldiers disguised as artisans, artists, heretical monks, actors and traders.

Spies under the guise of householders should bring to them weapons and armours in carts carrying wood, grass, grains and other goods, or in flags and images of gods.

Thereafter secret agents posing as priests, blowing their conch shells and beating their drums, should announce to the enemy that a powerful armed force of the enemy crazy to destroy all, is lurking closely behind them. Then amidst the consequent chaos and confusion, the spies should open the fort-gate and the towers of the fort to the army of the protagonist or disperse the enemy's army and kill them in the tumult.

The carrying over of troops into the enemy's fort is to be along with those moving in caravans or groups, with escorts, with those accompanying brides, with dealers in horses, with carriers of implements, with sellers or purchasers of grains, with those bearing the marks of monks and with envoys; peace is to be made during the period for creating confidence.

Seizure and Storming of Enemy's Fort

i) Setting fire to the besieged fort

Spies disguised as guards inside the fort, should place a fire-mixture in the tails of mongooses, monkeys, cats and dogs, and let them loose in stores of arrows, fortifications and houses.

Placing inflammable substances in the interior of dried fish or inside dried meat, the spies should bind these to the tails of birds and let them fly inside the fort.

Kauṭilya mentions various other means by means of which a besieged fort of the enemy could be set on fire. But, Kauṭilya warns that fire is a dangerous means to take a fort of the enemy. So whenever a fort can be captured by other means, no attempt should be made to set it on fire, because fire cannot be trusted. Fire destroys the people, grains, cattle, gold, raw materials and the like. Therefore, a fort captured by setting it on fire would mean the acquisition of a fort with its property all destroyed and therefore of very little worth to the conqueror.

ii) Secret agents, disguised as friends or relatives and with permissions and orders in their hands to meet friends or relatives inside the fort, may enter the enemy's fort and help to it captured by the protagonist as besieger. .

iii) A secret agent posing as an ally of the enemy should send mission to the besieged king to the besieged, "I am going to strike the besieging camp at such a time and place. Then you should also fight along with me."

When the enemy king agrees, the secret should show the tumult of an attack as mentioned and destroy him as he comes out of the fort at night.

iv) The spies of the protagonist should invite an ally or a forest chieftain in friendship with the besieged king, and entice him to fight against the besieged and capture his land. When any one of them falls into the trap of the spies and attempts to attack the enemy's territory, the enemy's people or the leaders of the enemy's traitors may be employed to murder him (the friend or the wild chief); or the assassin spies of the protagonist may kill him by poison.

Thereafter another pretending friend of the enemy should inform the enemy king that the murdered person was a fratricide (as he had attempted to seize the territory of his friend who is in troubles). Having acquired trust of the enemy, the spy pretending as friend should resort to deceitful means in order to sow the seeds of dissension between the enemy and his officers and have the latter hanged through insinuation.

v) Instigating through spies the peaceful people of the enemy to rise in revolt, the spies may put them down, unknown to the enemy.

Then having taken with him a portion of his army composed of furious wild tribes, he may enter the enemy's fort and enable the protagonist to capture it. Or traitors, enemies, wild tribes and other persons who have deserted the enemy, may, under the plea of having been reconciled, honoured and rewarded, go back to the enemy and allow the fort to be captured by the protagonist.

vi) A spy after securing trust of the enemy should get his brave warriors killed.

vii) After making peace with the enemy the protagonist should induce him to settle the country.

When settled, he should destroy the enemy's country.

viii) After inflicting harm on the enemy and thereby getting a portion of the enemy's troops led against treasonable persons or forest chiefs, the protagonist should capture the fort by a sudden assault.

Thus, according to Kauṭilya, the five means of taking enemy's fort are: secret instigation, espionage, drawing the enemy king out of the fort by trick, the act of siege and storming the fort.

Pacification of the Conquered Territory

According to Kauṭilya, after subjugating any country, the first and foremost task of the spy establishment would be to convince the people that the new king or his stooge is the friend of the people and bent on their welfare. Otherwise, the conqueror would always face oppositions and revolts from the people of the subjugated country. The spies should adopt all conceivable means to make people of the conquered country believe that the earlier ruler was inimical to them or incompetent and the new king has subjugated the country only to rescue the people from the torture or misrule of the earlier ruler/rulers. Kauṭilya prescribes the following measures to pacify the people of the conquered territory.

i) Spies should frequently propagate about the misconduct of the enemy king and the protagonist's love and regard for the chiefs in the country, towns, castes and corporations of the conquered territory.

ii) The protagonist king should try to win the hearts of the residents of the conquered territory through promises of looking after their customary rights, exemptions and protection.

iii) The protagonist should take prompt measures for honouring of all deities and hermitages, and make grants of land, money and exemptions to men distinguished in learning, speech and piety in the conquered land.

iv) He should order the release of all prisoners and render help to the distressed, the helpless and the diseased in the new territory.

v) The protagonist should ensure protection of wild life and domestic animals of the country conquered.

vi) He should ensure protection and security of the females in the new territory.

vii) He should abolish all unrighteous custom and practices and replace them by righteous ones.

viii) He should rearrange residences of people so as be convenient for both the king and the citizens and also to control activities of robbers, forest tribes and various other criminals.

ix) Information through spies about discontented persons, conspiracies against the protagonist, attempts at rebellion and riots etc. should be detected and suppressed accordingly.

Notes

1. Varuna = Hindu god of water, Nagas = mythical serpent gods

References

Lazo, Waleuska (2019): The Gift of Bravery: The Story of Eli Cohen - Our Hero and Spy, Waleuska Lazo, ISBN-1732743142, 9781732743144

About the Author

The author of this volume Dr. Ratan Lal Basu is a Ph. D. in Economics (on Arthaśāstra, the treatise on political economy and statecraft composed by a Brāhmaṇa scholar Kauṭilya around 300 B. C.). He retired as principal from a Government-Sponsored College at Kolkata, and after retirement got fully occupied with research and publishing activities pertaining to Indology, ancient economics, modern economic problems, economic history, yoga and tantra cult, statecraft, international relations and espionage, ethics and morality and also fiction in English and Bengali (his mother tongue).